INVOLUNTARY RESTRAINT

J. Renee North

Aunt Rachel -
You may be my Aunt, But
you're like a mom to me
too. Love you very much!
Johnna

J. Renee

PublishAmerica
PublishAmerica
Baltimore

First printing

ISBN: 1-4241-0385-1
PUBLISHED BY PUBLISHAMERICA, LLLP
www.publishamerica.com
Baltimore

Printed in the United States of America

Dedicated to:

Jonathan and Eric Hickman, my two wonderful sons, who put up with me working late on my book and being on the computer for hours, when they really wanted to be online themselves, or for me just to stop and go somewhere with them. Thank you both for your patience and for being the best kids a mom could ask for. I love you both.

I also would like to dedicate this to my sister Judy and my mother Kathleen. They were two of the most inspiring women I have ever known. They are both in heaven now, but even though I can't see them, they are with me always in my heart.

Introduction

I decided to write this book based on my own life experiences dealing with the every day life of living with panic attacks and anxiety. I was most inspired because through the years of having this disorder myself, I know what kind of treatment I received from people on the outside. This included my family members, friends, and anyone who knew I had this condition.

In this book I am going to be talking about things that many who have this disorder will be able to relate to. I am also going to be getting my point across to those outside the box, to those who don't understand what their loved one is going through and how they should deal with it. The only way I know about these feelings sufferers have—and to be able to successfully get the point across—is from referring to my own personal experiences of the ups and downs of dealing with panic in my life.

Chapter One
How It Began

My heart was pounding out of control and I couldn't breathe. The more I tried to catch my breath the worse I became until I was breathing so hard and so fast...

With one of my children in my arms and leading the other by his hand, everything began to go black before my eyes. I felt myself going down and all I could think about was that I was going to die; and then, there was only darkness. That was the most horrifying day of my life, and it was only the beginning of an ongoing living hell. This was my very first panic attack. For no reason, out of the blue, it just took over my body and I had no idea what was going on. My now ex-husband was in the military stationed in San Antonio, Texas. He was a medical specialist and worked at Ft. Sam Houston Medical Center. One afternoon while my husband was working, I had taken our sons to the commissary shopping center on post. All of a sudden, I started feeling very strange. I had never felt anything like it ever before.

I tried to shake it off and ignore it, hoping it would just go away, but it wasn't going to let me go. After I realized it was getting worse and my heart just kept beating faster and faster with every passing minute, I decided that I should go and take the babies to the hospital there on post where their dad was working. I didn't know what was going on, or what was happening to me, but I knew it wasn't good.

I didn't know anyone there in Texas where we were stationed. We had not been in the military very long and I had never been separated from my parents or siblings and friends back home. I was 1,300 miles away from everyone I knew except my husband, and his military duties came first. That is the way it is when you are in the military. It's kind of tough being a military wife. So I was totally lost without anyone to turn to.

All I remember thinking in the commissary when this feeling overwhelmed me was, "I must be having a heart attack." I left my cart right where it was, full of groceries. I grabbed up my kids and headed out the door to go to the car. By the time I got the kids in the car, I was fighting for every breath, feeling weak and disoriented. I managed to drive over to the hospital in a state of mind I can not even put into words. Finally I was there, and it seemed like I couldn't get to my husband fast enough. I got the kids out of the car and started up a pretty good flight of steps to the front door of the hospital. I remember looking at the steps and thinking, "My God, I will never make it to the top." As I started up the steps, I was in total panic. I could hardly move any part of my body by now. I was tingling all over and I just felt so weak. It was like my whole body was so heavy and trying to take a step was like trying to drag a bag of bricks tied to my ankles. I had never experienced such a strange and frightening feeling like this ever before.

I could barely keep myself moving. I stopped halfway up the steps and hung on the railing, trying to gain just a little more strength to try to make it inside the door. I thought if I could just get inside the hospital, someone would surely see me in the hallway and know I needed help. I proceeded to go one step at a time, until I finally reached the first set of doors into the hospital. It was kind of like a little landing area before going on into the next set of doors to the inside. I don't know how long it took me to get up there, but it seemed like forever and I had used all the strength I had.

Another lady was coming out of the hospital and I met her on the landing as I was going in. I must have looked pale, because she asked me if I was all right. If I looked as bad as I felt at that moment, I must have looked really bad! I told her that I was trying to get to my husband who was working in the recovery room of the hospital. As soon as I got that out of my mouth, I felt myself going to the floor. I passed out right there on the landing. I don't know what happened after I blacked out, but it was the nice lady, I was told, that took care of my babies and found my husband and got me help!

Chapter Two

In the Emergency Room

I woke up in the emergency room of the hospital where they poked my wrists with needles to draw blood from an artery to check my blood oxygen level. At that time they didn't have the nice little finger monitors like they do today. It seemed to me that I had been in the emergency room about two or three hours. I had finally come out of the attack and was feeling better, but I remember feeling really wiped out like I had run the longest marathon ever recorded in history. I was trying to wait patiently to hear what was wrong with me. I was ready for the worst! The doctor finally came to my bedside and he told me and my husband that what happened to me was just a panic attack and the reason I blacked out was because I hyperventilated, which means not getting enough oxygen to the brain. Now I'm thinking, *This doctor is crazy! I was having a heart attack, I know it. Just a panic attack?* At this point I know I had to have had that "confused look." I was totally dissatisfied with that diagnosis because I didn't know the first thing about panic attacks. I had never even heard of such a thing, and besides that, there wasn't anything going on for me to panic about. I was happy with my kids, happy in my marriage, and life seemed to be going well. I just didn't understand how the doctor could come up with that conclusion. It just didn't make any sense to me. So, I went home very confused and still pretty scared about what had just happened to me. I had never been afraid of much of anything in my whole life. But I was certainly afraid of having those attacks. I was afraid I was going to die.

I grew up a true tomboy and pretty much a daredevil. I could ride a dirt bike on the trails and jump the ramps with the best of the guys. I would ride the big roller coasters and go for drives and get lost just so I could find my way back, and I loved doing things like that. There wasn't much of anything that I was afraid to do, or at least try to do, and I could get in the car and go anywhere I felt like going, even if I had never been there before and didn't have a clue how to get there. I was a very outgoing person and enjoyed adventure, but my life suddenly changed and I became afraid of almost everything I had once enjoyed. I became tormented by these attacks that had suddenly taken over my body and mind. For no reason the attacks would come over me and all I could say was, "Oh my God, here comes another one."

This went on for quite a while. After that first attack, I would have an attack every day, and most of the time more than once a day. The doctor I went to see on post put me on some medication. When my mom heard about what was going on she bought an airplane ticket to come and stay with me to help me with the kids. She had never flown in an airplane before, but that wasn't going to stop her from getting to her little girl. Mom and I were very close, and I was the baby in the family, so I would always be her little girl.

Mom was there to go to the doctor with me for my next appointment. The doctor told my mom and my husband that I should go home to Ohio for awhile to be around people who could help me take care of the boys, and for me to try to get some counseling because he thought I was depressed. I didn't feel depressed; by this time I just felt petrified that I was going to die. The medication I was on kept me looped up until I really didn't care what was going on around me much. I wasn't myself at all while taking the medication, but it helped to calm me down, and I sure needed that! The panic attacks just wouldn't go away. There was no controlling them, and I was just a total nervous wreck. Thank God for my mom, who brought me home with her and helped me take care of the boys. I could barely keep my mind together to do anything, not even for my own self, so having the help with the kids was a blessing.

Chapter Three
In the Mind of Fear

I want to tell you what panic attacks done to my life, and how after fifteen years of suffering I was able to start doing some things that I hadn't been able to do because of this horrific debilitating disorder. If you are still reading this, I am going to assume that you have panic or anxiety attacks, or you know someone close to you who does. I need to tell you that I don't claim to have the miracle cure or know everything there is to know to get through your battle with panic attacks and anxiety. I only can share with you what I know and have learned through my own personal experience, and my own battle with panic and anxiety disorder. You should, by all means, consult a doctor if you haven't already, and let them do their professional work as well.

Sometimes it helps to know that others have felt the same way and have been through some of the same feelings that you have and can offer hope through their story. Maybe some of the things I have done to get my life back will help someone else get their life back, if not exactly like it was before the attacks began, at least enough that you feel you have a life to live for. By sharing my personal story and information, if I can help just one person change their mind and way of thinking, to save a lot of life long grief that doesn't have to happen, then it will be worth all the time and effort I am putting into this, and worth laying my life out on the table for the world to read about. I am not proud that I have had to live my life in bondage from panic and anxiety for so long, but I am proud of my accomplishments and the fact that I never stopped wanting to get my life back.

My goal is to help you understand what is happening to you. And to help others understand it too, so they might be able to put up with these crazy episodes you are having. It is a very trying time for everyone involved when you are dealing with something you can't explain. I am about to tell you what certain types of things made my life worse when others were trying to help, and what it really took to bring me out of it. I don't know how panic attacks have affected you and your everyday living. Maybe it hasn't been as bad for you as it was for me, but for a long time it was destroying my life and the lives of the ones I loved around me.

Panic attacks only get worse if you fear it. You can actually bring on an attack by being afraid of them and thinking constantly, *I know I am going to have another one, it is just a matter of time.* This is the way of thinking that almost destroyed my being in existence today. I was so afraid of having another panic attack that I couldn't think about anything else. I would walk the floor just waiting for an attack because I knew it was going to happen. Since the attacks would always appear out of the clear blue I wanted to be prepared. So I decided I was going to just be ready for it. I became totally paralyzed to this illness, and my life was consumed with waiting for a panic attack.

I was a very unhappy and fearful person who was bitter about what life had dealt to me. I became a real "female dog" to my husband, and my actions and the things that came out of my mouth during this trying time were absolutely not me. My marriage did not last and I believe it was because of how my disorder had changed me.

It has taken me a long time to get to where I am, and it was a pretty rough road to travel. For me to be able to recognize what was happening to me then, it grieves me now. Looking back, I see that I could have prevented all that bitterness that I allowed to build up inside of me from taking over my life. But I knew very little about panic attacks and anxiety, and knew no one that had the same problems I was having at the time. I felt like I had something no one else had ever had and nobody could help me.

I have often wondered if I would have had the opportunity to know more about this disorder when it first started, or knew someone else that had gone through it, maybe my life would have turned out differently. This is why this book is so important to me and why it is important that I be completely open about my own battle with panic and anxiety. My hope is that this will help someone else who is living day after day in fear, the fear of having another panic attack. If you are having problems with being bitter about life because panic attacks have paralyzed you like they paralyzed me, I am going to tell you something that is very important. I had to totally change my way of thinking, and I had to go out and face my fear before I could ever start getting any better. I will tell you more on what I did to overcome my fear later on in the book. Right now I want to tell you what happened to my life before I decided it was my life...or my life!

Chapter Four

The Walls Were Closing In

After my divorce from my boys' dad, it did not end there for me. Panic attacks are very frightening. They scared me so bad that I hated being alone for fear that I was going to die. Therefore, I searched for someone else to love me and take care of me because that was the only thing I knew to do for myself and my boys to have a home and stability. Panic disorder had a hold on my life so bad that I was making all kinds of bad decisions and choices. I went looking for security and stability in all the wrong places. I just knew that I wasn't stable or secure, and my kids needed and deserved both.

I was desperate. Everything I did was for my kids with the best of intentions, but it always came crashing down on top of me in a short period of time. My kids and I have moved so many times I can't count. I put them through so much trying to find something and someone to make me feel safe and good about myself. I always felt guilty because the boys' dad and I split up, and I was having these attacks and couldn't gain control of my life. I wanted to find someone to be with and give my sons stability with a mom and stepdad, and a home life of some kind. I just needed security in someone's arms. I thought that if I found the right person it would make everything OK.

For a very brief period, the panic attacks went away completely. We had been living with my parents, but since I was seemingly better, I got an apartment for me and the boys. About a year went by and the panic attacks came back. I went to my doctor and he told me that it was normal for the panic attacks to subside for a time and then come back. This was very discouraging news for me. I can't begin to tell you the way I felt the day I had another attack after being rid of them for almost a year. A feeling of doom came over me and then depression did in fact come into play in my life, and I knew I was depressed this time. I felt like I had just been played by the attacks, as they gave me just a little taste of freedom, only to return and take over my life worse than before. One way to put it would be that it's like a demon that comes in to destroy you and deceive you into believing that you are losing your mind. This was when it all started with the marriages and divorces, and moving from this home to another. It was no joyride, that's for sure. Not for me or my kids.

After the last marriage and divorce, something in me just clicked. I didn't want to need someone to take care of me in the way I had been thinking for so many years. I realized I had to work on myself and learn to love myself again, and to be happy. Most importantly, I had to learn to live with panic disorder one way or another, on my own.

Chapter Five

The Vicious Cycle

I was married and divorced four more times after my first husband. Yes, I know, I was getting right up there with the movie stars—ha ha. I am sure that panic attacks alone didn't cause all of my divorces, but I know they played a huge role in my failures in all of them in one way or another, and everything else in my personal life. Every aspect of my life was spinning out of control. The fear I had of being alone and having panic attacks were what drove me to feel like I had to be with someone. I didn't want to be alone; I needed security and stability that I couldn't give myself, or to my boys. I was still young. I didn't go out and trap men into marrying me nor did I just take whoever came along. I was picky, and every marriage I went into, I went into with full intentions of each lasting forever. I didn't cheat on any of them and I was faithful.

In spite of what many people think when they hear that I have been married and divorced five times, I honestly cared deeply for all of them and thought that I loved them at the time. I can honestly say that I care about all of them to this day still. Things would go pretty well until they got tired of dealing with my health issues and me not being able to work and pull my weight on the bills. It became a vicious cycle of being alone, finding someone, then getting hurt all over again because it never worked out.

With my first husband I was greatly saddened by that divorce. It literally made me sick. I lost so much weight that a size zero was too big for me. He was the only man I ever had children with, and that is a bond you can't ignore, no matter how you may despise them later on. The fact remained that I was not a well person and I could not be a good wife. Most men do not have the patience to deal with someone who is sick all the time. I wanted him to give me his undivided attention every second he was not at work. I was too demanding and clingy, and I know that helped to destroy that marriage. I didn't want him to go out with friends or do anything else. I just wanted him to be with me.

In 1995 I began to really think I had lost it. The attacks got worse; they were so bad that I was now house-bound. I did not go out of my house for nine months. The day I finally went outside was the day my mother took me to file for my third divorce. I had to sneak to get out of that one, as he became very verbally abusive to me—and to my kids. I thought if he knew I was going to try to get out, he would kill me for sure. In this marriage I was treated the way I was treating myself, which was like a whipped pup. I was totally dependent on him since I wasn't able to go out of the house. He did everything for himself and for me too.

I think he felt neglected because of my panic attacks and me being the way I was. This brought out a lot of anger in him and he became very controlling over me. My boys couldn't do anything right for him. They were only four and six years old, but they couldn't even eat at the table without him yelling. The yelling and screaming was just too much for me. My nerves could not take it anymore, especially on top of the panic attacks. I was just the nut case in the house to him. Between the remarks made and the lack of him not understanding, I strongly believe he was taking advantage of my illness as well; all of this only made my condition worse.

That was when I became housebound. Believe me when I say that those had to be the worst nine months of my entire life. I mean, panic attacks are bad but being afraid to go out of my house was awful! I didn't start getting any better until I got out of that situation. In the meantime, I lost all my close friends because I couldn't go out and do anything. I was so depressed I couldn't really talk to anyone on the phone, so slowly the life that I knew, the life that fulfilled me inside with great friendships and fun adventures, was dwindling down to nothing and no one.

Let me stop here and say this: yelling and screaming does not help someone with panic and anxiety disorder. If anything, it makes her worse. I still to this day cannot stand yelling and screaming and fighting. I like peace and harmony as much as I can have it. That is not to say that I get that all the time. I have just learned to deal with it when I have to, peacefully. Don't laugh. I really try to deal with it peacefully. I simply just remove myself from that kind of situation. Fighting may be healthy for some people, but it's not healthy for me. So, I'll just go on my way and leave them to do whatever they have to do. Eventually, they will notice that I am gone.

Everyone thought I was ignoring them and being stuck up because I wouldn't go out and do anything anymore and I didn't even like talking on the phone. The fact was I was just a basket case. None of what was going on in my life was what I wanted; it was something I could not control, and people didn't understand that. At this point I had it in my mind that this was going to be my life, and I would just have to get used to it. I didn't think I was ever going to get any better. When you can't do anything but sit around and try to not have a panic attack but end up having them anyway, you have a lot of time to think and feel sorry for yourself. You think about how you have been stripped of your life and of your freedom to go and do things and enjoy it without fear. Now you have fear in everything you do, everywhere you go. It is a horrible life; I know that because I have lived it.

I tried really hard to fight it, to try to be normal the best that I could. People would say things like, "For heaven's sake, what is wrong with you?" or "That is crazy to be that way!" They meant no harm in their words, but what they didn't realize is what it did to me every time someone would say anything to me about not being able to go here or there, or do this or that. The only thing those comments did for me was help in making me feel even more worthless and stupid, but no matter how worthless and stupid they made me feel, I could not control the attacks from taking over.

The most frustrating thing was not being able to make the people closest to me understand just how horrible these things were and how real they were. I didn't have support from anyone. The kind of support they wanted to give seemed to me like they were trying to shame me into getting better and into fighting back to being the person I had always been before. I wasn't in any shape to be taking a scolding from anyone. I was on guard all the time, and everything anyone said only made me even more bitter and angry that my life was being invaded by something I could not control.

Once my divorce was final I began to work on myself. I began to be able to get outside and I'd go in a car if someone else was driving, but they had to promise me that they wouldn't take me anywhere out of town because I didn't like being on country roads. That would throw me into a panic attack real fast. Country roads and the highway made me feel like I was in a place I couldn't get out of; I felt trapped, and it would make me feel like I was losing my mind. If I happened to be in a car and had a panic attack I would literally go crazy. I'd roll the window down and hang my head all the way out, all the while screaming for them to go faster to get me back into town, where I felt safe. I felt I had to be in my safe zone or I was going to die. I just could not control this overwhelming fear.

So, everyone knew better than to take me out on country roads or the highway where we could not turn around if needed. They all thought I was crazy, and I guess I can't blame them for thinking that way. I suppose if I was in a car and passed someone who had almost their whole body sticking out the side window, screaming "Go faster, go faster!" I'd think they were crazy too, or at the very least being very stupid. The fact is, it was stupid. It was dangerous for me to hang out of the car like that, but when you are in a state of panic you do things and say things that you would not normally do or say because it is a state of mind that you are in at the time. Later on I will be talking about mind over matter strategies that I use that help me in my decision making each and every day.

Chapter Six

The Disability Stage

By now I was with my fourth husband. I was doing somewhat better. I had a job and was working, but I knew my limitations. I had OK days, and then I had terrible days. So, I wasn't very dependable on the job. I had built up my safe zone to go where I had to go after I was able to drive again. Before I got to the point to where I could drive myself places, I would go to work two hours early because my husband at the time would take me before he went to work himself. If you have panic attacks, you know what your safe zone is. If you don't know what it means, I'll try to explain it to you. Safe zones are the places you know that you are able to go and still feel safe so you won't have a panic attack. My safe zone was at work and at home. When I was able to drive, I would go certain routes through town to get to work, and the places I needed to go, like the grocery store or Wal-Mart. The roads I took had to be the same roads every single time I went, so my driving was very limited.

I started having more bad days than good days. I became so paralyzed by the panic attacks that I could not hold a job. I tried very hard, but there were many days that I didn't make it off the couch to get to work, and I could not be dependable to be there. At this time, I had also been diagnosed as having Fibromyalgia. This is a skeletal muscular disorder; this too is caused by imbalances having to do with the serotonin in the brain. It causes a lot of pain all over your body. It is not life threatening, but it is not curable. You can only use pain management to keep the pain under control.

When I was about sixteen years old I was diagnosed as having Raynaud's syndrome. This is when the arteries collapse in your extremities when you get too cold or too hot, and the outcome of being in that type of environment is that you could lose a limb such as fingers and toes and possibly hands and feet. In middle school it was discovered that I had a curvature of the spine which is called scoliosis. Now I had all of these things going on in my body. I had a lot of pain from it all working against the other with my bones and muscles. This caused my panic attacks to accelerate due to the pain. So, the big thing is that my panic disorder started out being caused by one chemical imbalance, but now it's been aggravated by the chemical imbalance that causes the Fibromyalgia, and the pain that comes with it. So I found myself fighting all of these disorders all at once. Needless to say, my panic attacks were really out of control once again. After they diagnosed me with Fibromyalgia on top of everything else I was struggling with, I had to go on disability.

My family is all pretty much filled with the kind of people that believe in working hard. I like to call them workaholics. There's nothing wrong with having that kind of work ethic. I actually think it is a very good trait. When I was younger, before I started having panic attacks with the other illnesses, I could work like that too, and I actually miss being able to work outside the home. I enjoyed being with other people and learning things. But a few of my family members and some of my friends really wiped my face in the dirt about the fact that I wasn't working and was getting disability. This made me feel very worthless. I feel it is very important, to me, and to basically everyone, to do something with his life that he can feel good about. I feel that this book is just one of many that I will write because this is what I have found to be what I truly enjoy doing, and I think I do very well at expressing myself in words. This is also something that I can do and take a break whenever I need to. It is quite therapeutic for me as well. So, I encourage you to find something you are passionate about to work on. It will be very rewarding for you emotionally.

I was thirty-seven years old when I had to go on disability. You can't even begin to imagine what kind of abuse I went through because of that. I have learned not to let everything everyone says bother me so much. It is because of their lack of understanding and knowledge on this disorder that makes people ignorant to the fact that we, the panic-stricken people in the world, can't help it that we have been plagued by this illness. My mother used to tell me, "Don't make slurs or make fun of people with disabilities or illnesses they can't help, because the good Lord just might strike you down with the very thing you make fun of."

I found myself wanting so badly to tell people how I felt and how the comments made me feel, but I couldn't find the words. Having the problems I had were so embarrassing that all I wanted to do was avoid any conversations about it with anyone. I felt worthless in about every area of my life, and I knew that most everyone felt the same way about me as well.

Chapter Seven

Panic Attacks and Suicidal Thoughts

This is how I thought and felt at the lowest point in my life. See if you can relate to these thoughts.

I am going to be trapped inside this ball of panic forever. It's like being in a prison. The barred door is closed and locked, and the key, the key is somewhere. But where can I find it? How can I find the key to get out of this prison? I don't know where to look or who to ask for directions anymore. Everyone thinks I'm crazy, and lazy, and worthless anyway so what's the use. I'm no good for anything or anyone. I can't even be a good mother to my kids because I am in prison and I can't get out. I know there is nothing to be afraid of, yet everything scares me. Yes, I must be crazy. I've been hurt in the past, this happened and that happened, they think this about me, they said that about me, my life is messed up and I can't fix it. This is no life anyway, so I might as well just be dead.

I had reached my lowest point. This was probably my ninth or tenth year of dealing with panic attacks. I didn't have the will to fight it anymore. I just wanted to die. I felt like my life of living in fear and afraid to go out of my house—for fear of having a panic attack, not able to get to work or do most things normal people could do—was no life worth living. I couldn't be a good mother; I couldn't do anything for my kids outside of my house. If they missed the bus for school, it was a major crisis because I couldn't drive to get them across town to school. They either had to stay home or would have to go to school late. That was, if I had the money to put them on the dial-a-ride bus to get them there late. Oh, yes, it was a huge ordeal if my kids missed their bus for school.

I want to say my kids are a very big reason for me being where I am today. I felt like they were all I had to live for, but there was a time that I felt like they would be better off if I wasn't around. In reality I never wanted to leave them, so I just kept trying to hang on to some kind of hope to get through this battle. Panic and anxiety are very real and very scary and a very big pain in the butt to live with, but you can control them from taking over your life.

Panic and anxiety will make you think that there is no way out and no hope that you will ever be able to live a normal, fulfilled and happy life again. This is not true. I believe this only because I've done it and my accomplishments are such a big deal to me. It doesn't matter how small they are, they are massive to me. Those of you reading this that are paralyzed with this disorder. If you have made any strides forward, you know what I am talking about when I say they are big accomplishments. So, if you are laying on the couch, or in your bed, staying in your pajamas all day with no will to even get dressed or take a shower, keep reading this book. I want to help you get motivated to start toward taking your baby steps to getting out of your bondage of fear and anxieties.

Chapter Eight

Overcoming Panic Bondage

When I first accepted the fact that I was suffering from panic disorder and not having a heart attack was after I went to the doctor, about nine years after my first attack in Texas, and they ran tests on my heart. This was after several visits to the emergency room with my heart rate beating over 200 beats per minute, beating so hard and so fast that it literally shook my whole body inside and out. I was shaking out of control because I was letting my mind freak me out, thinking I was surely going to feel my heart burst and it was going to stop beating at any moment. This caused me to be more frightened and would throw me into hyperventilation which then made everything spin out of control.

The first thing I can recommend for you to do is have the tests done to ease your mind and confirm that you are truly having panic attacks and not a heart attack or something else you may think is going on. The mind will make you think of every possible thing in the world that it could be, and make you believe it is something life threatening. The mind needs to be at rest. It needs proof, so to speak. It was only when I did this that I was able to accept the fact that I was really having panic attacks and I was not going to die.

Having a panic attack won't kill you; it just makes you feel like you are going to die. To me, that is bad enough! After you have done your research and gone through all the tests and are able to conceive the fact that you are suffering from panic attacks, there is no time like right then to start learning how to control the fear it still produces in your life. It took me several years to start working on this in my life, but I didn't have someone tell me that I could do this. So, I'm telling you, you can control this. Don't wait until half of your life is over like I did.

To accomplish this, you are going to have to change your way of thinking about your condition. This worked for me, so it is worth a try for you too. I will start out by saying that doing this will take time and a lot of patience from your family and friends, and most importantly patience and determination in you. You will need someone you feel understands somewhat of what you are going through to support you and be your cheerleader. Your cheerleader is the person you can unload on when you have a bad day and someone who will rejoice with you when you accomplish even the smallest task of moving forward. This person will never make fun of you, or tell you negative things. She will be a good listener and won't judge what you have to say no matter how stupid it may sound. He must be a sincere person who realizes that you need his understanding and takes your condition as a real problem and not something in your head. This person will cheer you on to every baby step you take forward.

All you need is a little encouragement—and maybe even a lot of encouragement—but with this wonderful mental tool, I believe you can succeed because I have gone farther than I thought I ever would again by doing just what I am talking about here. So, you think about who this person might be for you to have as your cheerleader. Remember, they must *want* to do this for you. It will not be easy for either one of you during this process.

For me this happened to be a very good friend of mine whom with I had met doing some personal business. We kind of just instantly clicked and began talking to one another about different things. At that particular time in my life, as our friendship grew, I was going through a lot. I had accepted that I had panic disorder but I had no clue to what to do to help myself. I was just living one day at a time and dreaded the daytime, when my eyes would open and I would have to get out of bed and face yet another day of fighting off these attacks.

Before I met and became good friends with this person, who I refer to as "my Angel friend from God," I was totally dependent on my parents. However, my mother, who is now in heaven, was very sick with Lupus, and she was getting worse. I was very much attached to my mother; she was a wonderful Christian woman, and not just because she was my mom but because of the life she lived in front of me all my life. I had great confidence in her prayers. I knew if anyone could get a prayer through to God Almighty, it had to be my mother.

At this point in my life, all I had in the way of any hope at all was my mom's Prayers. I was still searching for that special someone to fill the void in my life, and I found him. Once again, I was trotting down the aisle thinking this was my answer for sure this time. But that marriage came to an end after only six years. During this marriage, one day while visiting my parents, I was called to the kitchen table to hear my mom and dad tell me that they were going to move to Tennessee. They really didn't give me a reason except to say that there were better doctors in Tennessee that knew about Lupus.

Needless to say, I cried, I begged, and I pleaded for them not to leave me, but in spite of all my tears and all my begging, they were going to go anyway. I was not fond of the idea of them leaving and not being able to see them every day. I was very close to my parents, and the thought of them not being near scared me beyond belief. I felt like I was back in Texas, so far away from anyone who provided me with any comfort or safety.

Two and a half years later, my mother passed away at Knoxville Baptist Hospital. I was devastated. Later my dad told me that my mom had asked him to take her away so I could get used to not seeing her and having her around every day. She was a smart woman, but it was the hardest thing I ever went through in my life. To this day I think of my mother as just being in Tennessee, and one day I will be able to go visit her again and hear her laugh, and hear her pray beside her bed, as I had heard many times through my years of growing up. It is the way I deal with her absence, and although it may not be the best way, it works for me.

I am convinced that my mom's prayers sent my Angel friend to me because God knew I was going to need someone. I had already thought about suicide several times, and even tried to do it—without success—because my mind was tired of fighting anxiety, and thinking about things that had happened in my life. I also didn't know if I could stand to live without my mother. She was my rock.

This friend of mine gave me a lot of things to examine in my life. She was a very wise person and I listened to her advice. Along with the advice, she was also there for me if I needed her for anything. But she helped me find the "want" to try to live again and to fight with all my might to get my life back and out of this fear that had hold on me. She was the cheerleader I needed for that extra boost of confidence that eventually got me out of thoughts like, *I'm giving up, I am just going to put myself out of this misery and then I'll be fine and out of everyone's way.* I felt I wouldn't be a burden anymore to my kids or a shame to my family and friends if I would just disappear.

My Angel friend convinced me that I needed to seek out

counseling with someone who could see things from a professional point of view. She was just a great friend that would nudge me, ever so gently, always with kind understanding words, to do what I needed to do to get out of my shell and stop living in fear. Step by step, she was with me all the way.

This is the message I want to get across to the people who are "outside of the box" and thinking that we are just mental cases and hypochondriacs. Believe me when I tell you, there is no one that wants to be better and free of panic attacks and anxiety than the ones who suffer from them. You can sit and make fun, judge, and ridicule until you are blue in the face and it will not help anyone. In fact, it makes it worse because they begin to think that they are worthless and have no reason to be in this world.

I am sure that my friends and family didn't know that they were doing this to me, but I hold no hard feelings against any of them because they just didn't have the knowledge to even begin to understand what was happening inside of me. I hope that people will read this and know that if they are doing this to their loved one or friend and trying to help them, what is really happening is that they are only feeding them negative thoughts to ponder on and eventually believe, while they continue to sit and fight this battle alone.

Once you have made it this far and have admitted to yourself that you have panic attacks, find someone you can trust and someone you are comfortable with to be your cheerleader. You can choose a friend, family member, counselor or your pastor. After you have done all that, then you have taken the first steps to becoming free of fear in your life. These people are only there to boost your "get up and go after it" side. The rest is up to you. I know that sounds scary and I won't tell you that it isn't. One of the things I had to overcome in my life of panic was first to step outside of the house, and then I had to get back to living. I'll give you a personal example of how my cheerleader helped me.

Driving my car frightened me, and even riding as a passenger sometimes I would panic instantly. But one day my Angel friend told me to get out there and start driving my car. She said go a little farther each day until you can go where you need to go. I was running her ragged by having her drive me every place I had to go. That is all it took for me. Just her little piece of advice was good enough; because the trust had been built between us, I trusted what she said to be Bible true. So, I began to drive a little distance at a time. The first time I drove my car after not being able to drive at all. I backed it out of the driveway and parked it on the street right in front of my house…WOW! Laugh out loud now. I know you want to. I admit, I didn't go very far at all but I felt like I had performed something wonderful. Yes, it sounds silly and I can laugh about it now but it wasn't a laughing matter then.

Each day I went a little farther, facing the fear that brought on the panic attacks. Every day I would get in my car and drive a little farther just here around my house. One day I made it around the block and what a day that was. I was so happy and proud of myself. Eventually, I got my encouragement up enough that I decided one day that I would drive my car up to my Angel friend's house. Now I had not been out on the roads for quite some time so this was a huge step.

I accomplished that goal that day and from there on I just kept inching out little by little being able to go all over my hometown. I am able to drive myself anywhere in town and I can drive anywhere if I have someone with me. I still won't drive out of town alone, and I still hate country roads whether I am with or without someone. I can usually go even though I don't like it, but I prefer the highway over country roads any day. I will never give up trying new things though. You will feel like a million bucks every time you reach a new goal in facing a new fear. Make sure you share that accomplishment with your cheerleader. Cheerleader, make sure no matter how silly it seems to you, you cheer the biggest and loudest and the most sincere cheer that you can for this person. It gives her encouragement to go out and keep moving forward every day to take another baby step further into her freedom of fearing panic attacks and anxiety.

Chapter Nine

Gaining Control

There's only one person who can gain control over your life. You guessed it, it is you. I can tell you what I have done and I can give you the details of how I overcame obstacles in life, but you have to be the one to see what works for you. Set your mind to regain your freedom to live and be happy and not be in bondage with panic and anxiety anymore.

Here is a newsflash! I may still have panic attacks every now and then, but the difference between now and then is that now the panic attacks don't have me. What I am saying is that I don't sit around and wait for one to happen anymore. I don't worry that one is going to hit me any minute, and I don't let panic attacks keep me from doing many things that I really want to do. If I really want to do something bad enough, then I know what I have to do.

I want you to pay close attention to what you are reading next. This is what I did, and still do, to gain freedom from my panic attacks. If you want to try this it may help you too, but I encourage you to have a backup plan if you do. I don't want to be responsible for telling anyone to go out and do this and they will be fine. I can promise you, if you face your fear like this, you will have a panic attack. You just have to remember that it will go away and you will be all right; you will not die from a panic attack.

The secret to this is to fight through it. Don't run back. Go on through, and keep your mind focused on only going forward. I don't care if I have to stop fifty times to go one mile. I know I can never go backwards if I want to beat the fear. Most of the time when I am facing a new fear, I will have to stop after going so far into the realm of fear, and then when I start feeling better in that place, I start again right where I stopped. If I let myself get freaked out and start turning around and going back into my safe zone, then I never get through it.

Once I get through it one time, then it becomes part of my safe zone as well. If you think you might freak out going through a panic attack to face a fear, you need to figure out a way to do this and still know you will be OK. For instance, if I am going out on a new face-my-fear day, I always take a cell phone with me. I do this because I know if I start freaking out all I have to do is call someone and talk to them about anything except that I am having a panic attack. I might mention the fact that I am not feeling very well, but then the subject needs to change to get my mind off of what I am feeling. I don't want to talk about having a panic attack, because I feel it means I'm giving the panic attack credit for making that call. It might sound weird, but I'm not giving credit to any panic attack for anything.

Why? Because my faith played an important role in helping me regain my life back. However, I also feel that my faith and beliefs also played an equal role in the cause of me being fearful most of my life. I believe—being part of the Christian community—panic and fear comes from a spirit of fear. Therefore, I look at panic attacks as being a demonic spirit of fear.

Chapter Ten

My Faith in God

As you have probably noticed by reading this far, I am pretty direct and to the point as to what I want to say and what I want to get across. This is no different in how I feel about my personal faith in God. I will make no bones about my faith. I believe in the Father, the Son, and the Holy Spirit. This is called the Trinity for those of you who don't know. God is the Father, Jesus is God's only Son, born of a virgin and conceived by the Holy Spirit, which is God's Spirit. I believe that God created man and woman from the dust of the earth, breathed his spirit into Adam and Eve and brought life into existence. So, that leaves me to being an heir to God the Father, because somehow I think we are all related to one another through Adam and Eve. It is mind blowing to try to figure out all the questions that even Christian Bible Scholars have about, How God became God, and when did he become God? The answer to that is that God has always been. He has been in existence forever. Forever is a very strong word because our minds can not comprehend it, no matter how hard we try. I have sat and tried to understand and figure out forever, and it is scary to me. It's something you just can't understand or even imagine. It is not possible, because in life on earth, we are in the flesh but we have that spirit inside of us. The spirit is what lives forever. Yes, there is that word again—*forever.*

I believe once we are conceived we live forever. After we die here on earth, we are not really dead. Our bodies are dead, but our spirit is alive somewhere. I believe somewhere is either heaven or hell. I don't believe there is any place in between heaven and hell, except for Earth, nor do I believe in reincarnation. So, I guess you could say, I see things in either black or white. When it comes to my faith, there are no grey areas to save us. This is how I was raised.

I was raised in the Church of God Cleveland Assembly. I attended for many years with my parents, so I have a lot of their teachings instilled into my heart and mind as a Christian. We had a youth pastor who was seven feet tall. Let me tell you, when he felt the spirit of God and decided to run a lap around the church in praise, we all got out of his way! Ha ha. But seriously, he was a very good man and I believe a true and sincere Christian. He was the head of our youth group called Pioneers for Christ.

I was very involved in the church. I sang in the youth choir along with about seventy other youth. Our choir director was the absolute best. When we went to the church to practice she would always give us this speech about how serious it was to sing in a church youth choir. We needed to walk the walk and talk the talk. We were to pray before we would sing for God to use us and send his spirit to bless the church through our singing. There wasn't anything fake about our choir director; she was also a sincere Christian woman, and I had faith in both of them and looked up to them as spiritual leaders, and still do to this day.

Growing up, most all my friends were from church, and all of our parents were one and the same. They were people who believed in heaven and in hell and if they had to scare us with the thought of us going to hell to get us to straighten up, then that is what they did. I'm not saying they were totally wrong in doing that. I love my parents very much, but the fact is, they used that scare tactics quite a bit with me. What I want to get across to you is that my faith, and the way I was brought up instilled fear in me at a very young age, fear of going to hell, fear of the rapture taking place and leaving me here alone. I also had a great fear in demons. I've told you all of this to tell you some true stories about my life and living in fear. Sometimes I think there are things that trigger panic attacks, and we don't even realize it.

My pastor was a powerful preacher. He didn't tip-toe around anybody, he preached straight from the Bible, and he preached on hell quite often. I remember one time in church we had a special evening of service. They were showing a movie called *The Burning Hell.* It was about people who died and woke up in hell. But they didn't die until someone had talked to them and tried to get them to give their life to Christ. The movie went right along with the Bible using the description of hell as it talks about in Revelations in the King James Version. The movie made it very real, and to a young Christian it was very scary.

In the movie, people that had known one another on earth were there in hell together. In one scene it focused on a Father and his Son. In hell, the son was with his Dad and he was screaming at him, telling him how he hated him because he had let him come to that horrible place. He blamed his dad for not taking him to church and showing him the way to heaven. They fought one another and gnawed on one another's flesh.

I remember seeing the worms crawling all over them, crawling up inside their nose and ears. Of course, the fire was all around them too burning their flesh to the bone. People were all over that fiery place and some were falling into the bottomless pit that looked like a volcano erupting down inside. They were screaming as they fell, and the screams seemed to last for miles until it faded away in the distance. It would show people stabbing one another with a sword and the sword would be all the way through the other person and the knife was twisted. You heard screams of excruciating pain, as the one stabbing the other would laugh the most demonic laugh I have ever heard. There were people begging for just one drop of water, others were begging to die, but the movie made it very clear that whether you went to heaven or hell, it was forever. There's that scary word again. I was about thirteen years old when I saw this movie. I will never forget it.

I honestly believe some of the things I was told and taught—like this movie—were at too young of an age. Not only did they scare me into being a good moral person and a person who believes in living right, but a person who in my subconscious mind became afraid of life itself. This very well could have been the reason I was always afraid of being alone, the reason for my panic attacks. Maybe it was the reason why I have been married and divorced so many times, for fear of growing old and being alone.

Notice how the word alone comes up so much in my statements? When someone has fear in her life, the last thing she wants is to be alone. Maybe the reason I was afraid to go out of my house for nine months was because in my subconscious mind I thought there were demons outside to hurt me. I could go on, but you get what I am saying here. Something triggers this fear in our minds. Sometimes we never figure out what it is but if you think really hard and research your life from childhood on, you might be able to identify what first started the fear in your life.

I know the medical point of view on panic and anxiety is that the cause is a chemical imbalance in the brain. I believe that, and I believe the medication helps that imbalance. I also believe that after we have experienced something tragic in our lives, our minds never forget it. This is where the mind over matter comes into place. The mind gets trained, either consciously or subconsciously, by every single thing that happens in our life from a very young age on. I believe I retrained my mind to think differently and more positively to be able to deal with this disorder.

Chapter Eleven

From a Medical Point of View

From all the doctors I have been to and from all the research I have done on my own to find out why we have panic attacks, anxiety, and other disorders, I've learned that panic attacks and anxiety—and other things like my Fibromyalgia—are caused by a chemical imbalance in the brain. In my research I have found that a chemical imbalance can affect people due to many things, such as change of life and hormones, puberty, and heredity. I even believe that some things in the environment can cause these disorders as well. Some of the things you can do to help yourself is to eat nutritious foods, get plenty of rest, and drink plenty of water. Also I have found that vitamin B6 helps me a lot. It is good to do research on your own but here are a list of different types of disorders and the definitions of the effects they produce. I found this information in several different places. This is just to help you identify what you may be feeling. If you identify the symptoms, you can help your doctor help you faster, and get you on the right medication and the right therapy as well. Doctors and medication are both very helpful. I encourage you again not to be ashamed to go to your doctor and take your medication. What I do want to get across to you is that along with the medical attention, you have to help yourself too.

Information

There are several different types of disorders:

-Social Anxiety Disorder

-Post-traumatic Stress Disorder (PTSD)

-Panic Disorder

-Obsessive Compulsive Disorder (OCD)

These are definitions for each disorder:

Social Anxiety Disorder:

If you have social anxiety disorder, you often get very nervous around other people. It feels like everyone is watching you and judging you. You're afraid of making a mistake or looking like a fool. You'll do anything to keep that from happening. You might even avoid certain people, places, or social events.

Post-traumatic Stress Disorder (PTSD):

If you have post-traumatic stress disorder or PTSD, you have lived through, seen or heard about a horrible or traumatic event. It made you feel scared, helpless or shocked, and you can't seem to get over it. The stress of a traumatic event causes chemical reactions in the brain and even physical symptoms. You might have nightmares. You might feel that the event is happening all over again. You might be jumpy and tense. You might even stay away from people or places that remind you of the event.

Panic Disorder:

If you have panic disorder, you suffer from sudden feelings of extreme terror. These are called "panic attacks." They could happen at any time. You might feel like you're in great danger or even think that you are dying or going crazy. You might worry about having an attack in a place that's hard to get out of. This can make you afraid to leave home.

Obsessive-Compulsive Disorder (OCD):

If you have obsessive-compulsive disorder or OCD, you're overwhelmed by disturbing thoughts you can't control. These are called obsessions. To get rid of these thoughts, you might do certain things over and over again, like check to see if the stove is turned off or wash your hands. These are called compulsions. If you don't do them, you feel that something bad will happen. You know it doesn't make sense, but you can't change this unwanted way of acting or thinking.

If you have any of these disorders, or know someone who does, it is important that medical attention is sought, because medication does help these disorders. However, the mind over matter strategy can still help overcome these thoughts if you practice it.

Chapter Twelve
Mind over Matter

A few things I want to mention also are some of the things that I have found to be very helpful in controlling my panic disorder. I seem to be more apt to having one if I am really tired or if I am in pain. Here are a few tips for you that may help you as well. First, I need to be scheduled, and especially in the area of sleep time. I need a certain time to go to bed at night, and a certain time to wake up. When I wake up, I need to have a routine set for myself. Also, getting some exercise helps as well so I try to slot a time in for that in my schedule. I can't say that I always follow this routine, but when I don't, I notice a big difference in the way I feel. I am more agitated and nervous and I know that I've messed up.

When this happens, I try to focus on other things and I try to take a leisure day and do things that are calming for me. For instance, playing the piano or guitar or reading a book. I like to play online games on the Internet too. Another great way to relax that I really enjoy is taking a nice warm bubble bath with candles and soothing music. Things like this help to relax my mind and my body.

You can do anything you enjoy that will get your mind thinking more positive thoughts rather than constantly thinking about the fact that you are feeling bad. For me, I know that eventually, if I don't get my mind thinking in a different direction, I will most likely have a panic attack. If I keep my mind on something else—something that is interesting to me and keeps my mind busy—it helps me to completely forget about stress and worry, which is the biggest thing I have found that brings my panic attacks on. So, you can control this fear of fear by keeping your mind set on things that make you happy or on something you are really interested in doing. I don't know if any doctor calls this a type of therapy, but it is great therapy for me.

Sometimes I talk myself through a panic attack by telling myself, "OK, this is nothing to get worked up about, it will go away and I am not going to die." When I do that, I'm going face to face with my fear of panic attacks and that is something that helps me more than anything. You can practice that whether you are taking medication or not. Medication only helps relieve the symptoms, it does not teach you to deal with the illness itself. Therefore, if you never come face to face with your fear, it will always be there and this is when it can take over your life. Don't run from a panic attack. Instead, face it straight ahead, and know that you are going be all right, and not let it scare you into thinking that it controls you. You have the ability to control your mind.

Remember when I said I had given up, and it was either my life or my life? This is when I talked to my cheerleader and told her I could not stand it anymore. Through her kind and gentle and understanding spirit, she helped me to decide to go back to the doctor. I had given up on doctors at this point. It had been around nine years by now, and I was only getting worse. The disorder had taken over my life; I had fought so long and so hard that I was so tired and all I wanted to do was die.

When I went into the doctor's office, I will never forget what I told him. I looked him in the eye and I said, "I can't live with these panic attacks any longer; I don't have a life, and if you can't help me, I am going home and blowing my head off." You can bet that got his attention. Ha ha! I often wonder why he didn't call someone up right then and there to send me off to a mental hospital, but he didn't. He then told me about the chemical imbalance that caused this disorder. He was very understanding and he knew I was desperate. He took the time to talk to me and give me information medically about why these attacks were happening to me, and that there was something that could help by way of medication. He put me on an anti-depressant. There are so many anti-depressants out there and what worked for me may not work for you, but that is something you have to go through with your doctor. That is one trial and error I can't help you with. The anti-depressant he prescribed for me helped me tremendously. I felt results in about a week. Sometimes, you just have to go and tell the doctor exactly how you feel. I, however, didn't get the anti-depressant I needed years ago when the panic attacks first started. I don't know if they knew everything they do now about different medications and I am not even sure that the one I am on had hit the market back then. It has been fifteen years of trial and error for me, but hopefully this information will spare you the errors I made, and you can begin to sail through to your own victory of beating the battle of panic attacks.

Chapter Thirteen

Life on Pause

There is something else that has caused this driven force inside me that just won't stop fighting, or dreaming, or wanting to live life to the fullest. I don't know about you, but I was tired of my life being on pause. When I got the right medication and I could finally go out of my house, I craved to go and do things. I had been so locked up inside, and now I just wanted to go and never stop. There was just one problem with that. I was still afraid to drive myself too far away from home.

Here's a perfect example for you. Let's say I want to go shopping today, and the mall is a whole ten miles down the highway. This means I can't go if I don't find someone to ride along with me. Can you guess what happens? Everyone just happens to be busy. Well, let's get real here. We really can't expect for people to always be there when we want them to be. Everyone has their own lives to live and just because we have this problem people are not going to put their lives on hold for us. This reality was very depressing for me, not because people weren't there for me when I wanted them to be, but because everything I wanted to do was always so complicated.

One day I started thinking how nice it would be to just get in the car and go to the mall. Just to have that kind of freedom back in my life would be so wonderful. People that can go anywhere they want, anytime they feel like, do not understand how this feels to us. After not being able to go anywhere, and being in that bondage of panic attacks, I don't take that freedom for granted anymore. I am so grateful for every single place I can now go, and every single thing that I can now do by myself. I almost feel like a five-year-old that has just learned how to tie her shoes. When she finally gets it, it's the most wonderful feeling in the world. That's exactly how I feel every time I take a new step into fighting my fear. I never realized myself, until I started having panic attacks, just how much it means being able to do the things we do every single day that most of us never give a second thought about doing.

Chapter Fourteen
Living Again

You can probably tell by my little laughs noted in some of my sentences that I have been able to regain my sense of humor. I love to laugh and be with friends and family. I don't take anything or anyone for granted anymore. I am very grateful that I am still alive and where I am today. I am thankful to God, most of all, for looking down and helping me find the strength to fight. For sending me a cheerleader and wonderful friend to give me encouragement to live and for letting me find the peace I have found, I thank Him. Instead of being depressed and dreading every day, I wake up to see the sunrise. Instead of being trapped inside my fear of the outside world, and instead of just thinking about being able to go shopping in my daydreams, I now look forward to the day I will have daughters-in-law to go shopping with, and grandbabies to spoil, and vacations I will take. I'd say that is a pretty good trade-off to be ever so thankful for.

I have had to endure a lot of pain in my life. But I have learned a lot through it all. I would have to say that it has made me a stronger person in many areas of my life. Although I wouldn't want to go back and relive this life all over again, I won't say that I am sorry I had to go through it. There was a purpose for me to go through all that I have. Therefore, to me, it was just part of my life.

We all have a parts of our lives that we are not proud of and maybe don't want to even think about, much less talk about, or write a book. But the truth is, we learn something valuable in the mistakes we make, or in the pain we go through. No matter what it is that we do in life, we will always be learning every single day how to make our lives better, or more fulfilled.

I hope my words and my story will encourage you to fight your way to freedom, and start living again. There's so much we have to live for and look forward to. It's been said before, and I have found it to be so true, that the older we get the faster the years go by. Before we know it, we will be older and unable to do some things we could have done when we were letting fear rob us of our lives. There is no time like right now, to get up and face your fears, face the dreaded feelings, face all that unhappiness in your life that makes you miserable and not able to enjoy living. Just decide that it has to go. Set your mind to the fact that you don't want to live like this anymore, and that you don't have to. Just know that whatever it is that you have to do for yourself to have your life back, you can do it.

As I come to the end of my story, I want to leave you with these thoughts to ponder upon as you go on your own journey to find freedom from fear, panic, and anxiety. You know you can fight it. You have just read about a person that has proven it to herself. Now it is time for you to prove it to yourself.

My motto for life is this: "Don't give up, and don't give in, just keep going." And most importantly, "Don't ever look back."

Printed in the United States
38740LVS00006B/496-543